POLAND 2016 HUMAN RIGHTS REPORT

EXECUTIVE SUMMARY

Poland is a republic with a multiparty democracy. The bicameral parliament consists of an upper house, the senate (Senat), and a lower house (Sejm). The president, the prime minister, and the Council of Ministers share executive power. Observers considered the May 2015 presidential elections and the October 2015 parliamentary elections free and fair.

Civilian authorities maintained effective control over the security forces.

During the year parliament passed a public assembly law, a counterterrorism law, a surveillance law, media laws, and laws related to the Constitutional Court which local and international nongovernmental organizations (NGOs) indicated may have a negative impact on human rights protection and the principles of democracy and the rule of law.

Among the country's principal human rights problems were xenophobic and racist incidents, including both hate speech and hate crimes involving violence, and cases of anti-Semitism. Local NGOs stated verbal harassment and physical violence targeting racial and ethnic minorities and foreigners increased. An increasing backlog of cases and lengthy court procedures impeded the delivery of justice.

Other human rights problems included abuse of prisoners and detainees by police, inadequate medical facilities and treatment in jails and prisons, compulsory hormone therapy to lower sex drive for some convicted sex offenders, and at times inadequate cell space and antiquated prisons. Delays in the restitution of private property continued. Criminal defamation laws restricted freedom of speech and press by discouraging speech, publications, and material on the internet critical of public officials. Official corruption remained a problem, despite enforcement efforts. During the year the government severely cut the budget of the office of the public defender for human rights and limited its ability to perform its functions. Burdensome procedures discouraged appropriate classification and treatment of domestic violence as a crime. Societal problems included discrimination against women in the labor market, abuse and sexual exploitation of children, trafficking in persons, restrictions on the ability of persons with mental disabilities to participate in civic affairs, and discrimination and violence against ethnic minorities as well as lesbian, gay, bisexual, transgender, and intersex (LGBTI) persons. Violations of workers' rights to organize and join unions and to strike as well as antiunion discrimination also occurred. The government did not always effectively enforce laws governing the work of minors between ages 16 and 18.

The government generally enforced human rights and took steps to prosecute officials who committed abuses, whether in the security services or elsewhere in government.

Section 1. Respect for the Integrity of the Person, Including Freedom from:

a. Arbitrary Deprivation of Life and other Unlawful or Politically Motivated Killings

There were no reports that the government or its agents committed arbitrary or unlawful killings.

b. Disappearance

There were no reports of politically motivated disappearances.

c. Torture and Other Cruel, Inhuman, or Degrading Treatment or Punishment

The constitution and law prohibit such practices. There were problems, however, with police misconduct and corrections officers' abuse of prisoners. The law lacks a clear legal definition of torture, which authorities did not report as a separate crime, but all actions that could be considered "torture" are prohibited and penalized under other provisions of the law. The law outlines disciplinary actions for police, including reprimand, demotion in rank, and dismissal. Civil society groups noted cases of police misconduct against persons in custody.

Investigation into abuse of power by 10 police officers in Olsztyn continued at year's end. In April 2015 prosecutors charged the officers with the use of violence and threats to extract testimonies from detainees. Through the end of September, prosecutors identified 30 victims of the crime.

The law gives judges the option of ordering compulsory hormone therapy for a person convicted of either rape or incest when the victim is younger than age 15. Judges may order the procedure for convicted pedophiles at any time up to six months before their expected release. According to justice ministry statistics, the courts ordered the procedure for 18 pedophiles in 2015 compared with 20 in 2014.

Prison and Detention Center Conditions

Prison and detention center conditions were adequate. Vacancies in the prison medical staff and limited prisoner access to specialized medical treatment continued to be problems.

<u>Physical Conditions</u>: While authorities generally separated juveniles from adults, the law allows shared housing in prisons and detention centers in exceptional cases. Juveniles were at times held together with adult prisoners. Authorities usually sent juveniles between ages 17 and 21 accused of serious crimes to pretrial detention.

Authorities often held pretrial detainees in prisons pending trial, but in areas separate from convicts. Conditions for pretrial detainees were generally similar to those for prisoners, but on occasion they were worse due to overcrowding and poorer facilities resulting from court-mandated restrictions on where a prisoner should be located while awaiting trial. A report by the Council of Europe's Committee for Prevention of Torture (CPT) pointed out in 2013 that an almost total lack of activities for pretrial detainees made their situation considerably worse than that of convicts. There was no indication the government addressed this problem.

The law sets the minimum cell size at 32 square feet per person, but prisoners may occupy smaller cells for a limited time. Both local NGOs and international organizations, including the UN Committee Against Torture and CPT, expressed concern that the 32-square-feet standard was not compatible with the European standard of at least 43 square feet per person in multiprisoner cells and 65 square feet in single-prisoner cells. As of the end of September, no detainees were in cells smaller than the legal minimum of 32 square feet, according to government statistics.

The Legal Intervention Center, a Warsaw-based NGO, reported that many prison buildings dated to the 19th century and were in need of substantial renovation. On October 28, the prison authorities opened a new prison unit in the town of Ciagowice, which can hold up to 275 persons. In November 2015 authorities closed a 170-year-old prison facility in the city of Kalisz. In 2013 the CPT found that authorities at the Municipal Police Department in Lublin, the Metropolitan Police Department in Warsaw, and the Warsaw-Bialoleka Police Department did not respect the privacy of communal toilets and showers. At the Bydgoszcz

Municipal Police Department, the closed-circuit television coverage included the in-cell toilets. These problems persisted.

During the first nine months of the year, 65 prisoners died in prison, including 15 reported suicides. The Helsinki Human Rights Foundation described systemic problems with medical care in prisons. These included inadequate medical staffing, such as a lack of specialized medical care, too few doctors to handle the workload, and poor medical infrastructure.

According to the human rights defender's report in July, most prisons and detention facilities did not meet the needs of persons with disabilities. Although prisoners with disabilities may be placed in cells modified for their disability, prisoners with disabilities had limited access to shower rooms, community rooms, and walking areas. According to the Helsinki Human Rights Foundation, prisoners with disabilities often complained about problems with moving around facilities, inappropriate equipment in the cells, and the need to ask cellmates for assistance with moving around.

The law permits authorities to commit prisoners to the National Center for the Prevention of Dissocial Behaviors who have served their prison sentences and undergone a custodial therapy program, but who have mental disabilities of a nature that a high probability exists they would commit another serious crime against a person. The Helsinki Foundation for Human Rights pointed out that mandatory detention after completion of sentence may violate the person's freedom and be retroactive. On November 23, the Constitutional Court ruled the law constitutional.

Administration: Authorities investigated credible allegations of inhuman conditions and documented their findings in a publicly accessible manner. The human rights defender may join proceedings in civil and administrative courts on behalf of prisoners and detainees, either when these file a complaint or when information otherwise leads to an allegation of inhuman conditions. At the request of the Ministry of Justice, the human rights defender administers the national preventive mechanism to investigate and monitor prison and detention center conditions. During the first nine months of the year, the ombudsman visited 12 prison and detention facilities, including pretrial detention centers and prison facilities. The Office of the Ombudsman publishes its findings and a summary of its recommendations to relevant authorities in an annual report.

<u>Independent Monitoring</u>: The government allowed independent monitoring of prison conditions and detention centers on a regular basis by local human rights groups as well as by the CPT. The Helsinki Human Rights Foundation and other local NGOs made occasional visits to prisons.

d. Arbitrary Arrest or Detention

The constitution and the law prohibit arbitrary arrest and detention, and the government generally observed these prohibitions.

Role of the Police and Security Apparatus

The police force is a national law enforcement body with regional and municipal units overseen by the Ministry of the Interior and Administration. The border guard is responsible for border security and combating irregular migration, and it reports to the Ministry of the Interior and Administration. The Internal Security Agency (ABW) has responsibility for investigating and combating organized crime, terrorist threats, and proliferation of weapons of mass destruction. The Central Anticorruption Bureau (CBA) is responsible for combating government, business, and financial corruption. The prime minister appoints the head and deputy heads of the CBA and supervises the bureau, which may investigate any matter involving public funds. The prime minister supervises the heads of both ABW and CBA, which also report to parliament.

On July 2, a new counterterrorism law designated the ABW as the primary authority for combatting terrorism and increased its law-enforcement powers. On July 11, the human rights defender referred the law to the Constitutional Court, arguing it violates the right to privacy and freedom of communication, and is unclear on grounds for accumulating data on individuals, arresting civilians, banning demonstrations, disconnecting citizens from the internet, and for surveillance on non-Polish nationals without a court order. The case remained pending before the Constitutional Court at year's end.

Civilian authorities maintained effective control over the police force, the border guard, the ABW, and the CBA, and the government has effective mechanisms to investigate and punish abuse and corruption. There were no reports of impunity involving the security forces during the year.

Arrest Procedures and Treatment of Detainees

The constitution and the law require authorities to obtain a court warrant based on evidence to make an arrest, and authorities generally complied with the law. The constitution and the law allow detention of a person for 48 hours before authorities must file charges and an additional 24 hours for the court to decide whether to order pretrial detention. The new counterterrorism law allows authorities to hold terrorism suspect without charges for up to 14 days. The law sets a five-day limit for holding a juvenile in a police establishment for children if the juvenile escaped from a shelter or an educational or correctional facility. It allows police to hold for up to 24 hours in a police establishment for children a juvenile who is being transferred to a shelter or an educational or correctional facility, in case of a "justified interruption of convoy." The law provides that police should immediately notify a detained person of the reasons for his detention and of his rights. Usually this information is initially delivered orally; later, at the police station, the detainee signs a statement that he has been advised of his rights and duties. Police give the detained person a copy of the report on his detention. Authorities generally respected these rights. Only a court may order pretrial detention. There was a functioning bail system, and authorities released most detainees on bail. Defendants and detainees have the right to consult an attorney at any time. The government provided free counsel to indigent defendants. On January 1, a new law providing free legal counsel, including at the pretrial stage, to poor, young, and senior citizens, veterans, members of multichild families, and victims of natural disasters entered into force. Authorities did not hold suspects incommunicado or under house arrest.

Pretrial Detention: The law permits authorities to detain persons charged with a crime for up to three months. A court may extend pretrial detention every six to 12 months, but the law specifies that the total time in detention may not exceed two years, except in certain complex cases, when the court may petition an appellate court for an extension beyond two years. On January 8, the human rights defender referred to the Constitutional Court several provisions of the code of criminal proceedings that provide for the possibility of extending pretrial detention without specifying the maximum length of detention and without providing specific justification. The case remained pending at year's end. According to the Ministry of Justice, extension beyond two years may occur if criminal proceedings are suspended, there is a need to identify or confirm the identity of the detainee, a very complicated investigation must be performed outside the country, or the detainee purposefully prolongs the proceedings. As of June 30, authorities held five persons for longer than two years in pretrial detention.

<u>Detainee's Ability to Challenge Lawfulness of Detention before a Court</u>: Arrested persons are entitled to challenge before a court the legal basis or arbitrary nature of their detention within seven days of the court's decision.

<u>Protracted Detention of Rejected Asylum Seekers or Stateless Persons</u>: Authorities placed some asylum seekers in guarded centers for foreigners while they awaited deportation or decisions on their asylum applications. Border guards may place an individual in a guarded center only by court order. The law prohibits the placement of unaccompanied minors under age 15 in guarded centers. Border guards typically sought in this way to confine foreigners who attempted to cross the border illegally, lacked identity documents, or committed a crime during their stay in the country. According to the Helsinki Human Rights Foundation, border guards placed families with children into guarded centers.

e. Denial of Fair Public Trial

While the constitution provides for an independent judiciary and the government generally respected judicial independence, an increasing backlog of cases made the judiciary less efficient.

The court system remained cumbersome, poorly administered, and inadequately staffed. The consensus among local human rights NGOs was that the judicial system was improperly structured and inefficient, with a poor division of labor among different courts. Difficult hiring procedures created many vacancies among judges and support staff, and slowed the justice system. Judges were forced to do administrative work that staff would normally perform. Judges reported receiving an increasing number of cases, while the number of judges remained the same. A continuing backlog of cases and the high cost of legal action deterred many citizens from using the justice system.

On June 15, Nils Muiznieks, the Council of Europe's commissioner for human rights, in a report of his visit to the country from February 9 to 12, expressed concern that a new law granting extensive powers to the minister of justice without the establishment of corresponding sufficient safeguards to avoid abuse of powers, poses "a considerable threat to human rights in the context of criminal law procedures, including the right to a fair trial, the presumption of innocence and the right to defense." Another matter of concern to Muiznieks was the creation of a new department within the Prosecution Office responsible for prosecuting the most serious crimes committed by judges and prosecutors. He feared this reform's "potential chilling effect of this on judges and prosecutors and the ensuing negative repercussions on the independence of the justice system."

The country employs an "e-court" to adjudicate simple cases, which typically involve unpaid utility bills. A party may file a civil claim for monetary damages on the e-court's website, and a judge may issue a writ of payment based on the electronic submission. Defendants who dispute the judgment have recourse to a regular court for trial.

Trial Procedures

The constitution provides for the right to a fair public trial, and an independent judiciary generally enforced this right. Defendants enjoy a presumption of innocence and the right to prompt and detailed notification of the charges against them, with free interpretation for defendants who do not speak Polish from the moment charged through all appeals. They have the right to a fair and public trial without undue delay and the right to be present at their trial. Trials are usually public, although the courts reserve the right to close a trial in some circumstances, including divorce proceedings, cases involving state secrets, and cases whose content may offend public morality. Defendants have the right to legal representation, and indigent defendants may consult an attorney provided without cost. The government must provide defendants and their attorneys adequate time and facilities to prepare a defense. They may have access to government-held evidence, confront and question witnesses, and present witnesses and evidence on their own behalf. Prosecutors may grant witnesses anonymity if they express fear of retribution from defendants. The prosecutor general may release to the media information concerning any investigation, except if such information is classified, with due consideration to important public interests. Defendants may not be compelled to testify or confess guilt.

After a court issues a verdict, a defendant has seven days to request a written statement of the judgment; courts must provide a response within 14 days. A defendant has the right to appeal a verdict within 14 days of the response. A two-level appeal process is available in most civil and criminal matters.

The law extends the above rights to all defendants.

Political Prisoners and Detainees

There were no reports of political prisoners or detainees.

Civil Judicial Procedures and Remedies

Individuals or organizations may seek civil remedies for human rights violations. The government's implementation of court orders, particularly for payment of damages, remained slow, cumbersome, and ineffective.

After they exhaust remedies available in the domestic courts, persons have the right to appeal court decisions involving alleged government violations of the European Convention on Human Rights to the European Court for Human Rights.

The dispute regarding judicial appointments to the Constitutional Court continued throughout the year. In March the court struck down in its entirety the December 2015 law regulating its operations. The government boycotted the court's proceedings and refused to publish the ruling as required by the constitution. The European Commission and the Council of Europe separately criticized the government's actions. The Council of Europe's European Commission for Democracy through Law (the Venice Commission) criticized the government's refusal to publish the court's ruling.

In July the government passed legislation regulating the court's operations that addressed some of the Venice Commission's concerns. In August the court struck down some provisions of the legislation in a ruling the government again refused to publish. In October parliament introduced additional legislation regulating the conduct, immunities, and discipline of court judges. Opposition parties, academic and legal experts, the Helsinki Human Rights Foundation, and other NGOs stated aspects of the legislation of December 2015 and July 2016 impeded the court's operations and violated the constitutional principles of judicial independence, separation of powers, and checks and balances among the branches of government. The government argued it was working to resolve the situation and published all court rulings issued during the year up to July 20, except for the March ruling on the court legislation. In July the European Commission issued a rule of law recommendation for Poland criticizing certain aspects of the government's July legislation, and the Venice Commission issued a new opinion in October along similar lines. On November 7, the Constitutional Court ruled constitutional the article from the July legislation altering the selection process of the chief justice. Three judges refused to participate in the hearing, and the ruling was issued by a five-judge panel despite the July legislation requirement of a full court panel hear all cases governing the operation of the court. The government had not published the ruling by year's end. On December 19, the president signed a new law regulating the conduct, immunities, and discipline of court judges, and establishing new procedures for court leadership. On December 21, he swore in a new chief judge selected under the law's new procedures. Also on December 21, the European Commission issued a complementary rule of law recommendation stating the new law addressed some issues raised in the July recommendation but that some rule of law concerns remained, and that the new law also raised new rule-of-law concerns regarding the effective functioning of the Constitutional Court and constitutional review of legislative acts.

Property Restitution

The law provides for restitution of communal property seized during the Communist and Nazi eras, but the process proceeded very slowly during the year. By the end of September, the property commissions resolved 6,854 of slightly more than 10,500 communal property claims.

No comprehensive law addresses the return of or compensation for private property, but individuals may seek the return of confiscated private property through administrative proceedings and the courts. On August 17, the president signed into law legislation protecting Warsaw public properties from being returned to their precommunist era owners and extinguishing long-dormant claims after a six-month notice period if no claimant steps forward to pursue a restitution case. The legislation was intended to end abusive practices in the trading of former property owners' claims but raised serious concerns that it fell short of providing just compensation for former owners who lost property as a result of nationalization of properties by the communist-era government. The Constitutional Court upheld the legislation, and the law entered into force on September 17.

f. Arbitrary or Unlawful Interference with Privacy, Family, Home, or Correspondence

The law prohibits such actions but allows electronic surveillance with judicial review for crime prevention and investigation

On February 3, the president signed a new law regulating police and security services surveillance in response to a 2014 Constitutional Court ruling that held as unconstitutional several provisions of the laws giving law-enforcement agencies and special services broad access to telephone records. On February 18, the human rights defender referred the law to the Constitutional Court arguing it infringes privacy rights and EU data privacy norms and does not provide sufficient protections for privileged communications (e.g., attorney-client, priest-penitent). At year's end, the case was pending before the Constitutional Court. An opinion by the Venice Commission issued June 13 commended the government for improving existing surveillance law and practices but criticized some aspects of the new law.

Section 2. Respect for Civil Liberties, Including:

a. Freedom of Speech and Press

While the constitution provides for freedom of speech and press, laws restrict these freedoms. In the past the government and courts upheld laws that criminalize defamation by individuals and the media and limit editorial independence.

Freedom of Speech and Expression: The law prohibits hate speech, including the dissemination of anti-Semitic literature and the public promotion of fascist, communist, or other totalitarian systems.

Press and Media Freedoms: On May 13, the coordinator for special services, Mariusz Kaminski, announced before parliament's Special Services Committee that during the previous government the ABW and the CBA had 52 journalists under surveillance. The former heads of the two agencies denied these allegations.

Censorship or Content Restrictions: The constitution prohibits censorship of the press or social communication. At the same time, the law prohibits under penalty of fines the promotion of activities against government policy, morality, or the common good and requires that all broadcasts "respect the religious feelings of the audiences and, in particular, respect the Christian system of values." The government rarely enforced this provision. The law also places some limits on editorial independence, for example, by specifying that journalists must verify quotations and statements with the person who made them before publication.

The National Radio and Television Broadcasting Council, a five-member body appointed by the Sejm (two members), the senate (one member), and the president (two members), is constitutionally responsible for protecting freedom of speech and has broad power to monitor and regulate programming, allocate broadcasting frequencies and licenses, apportion subscription revenues to public media, and impose financial penalties on all public and private broadcasters. While council members are required to suspend their membership in political parties and public associations, critics asserted that the council remained politicized.

Local and international NGOs raised concern regarding recent legislation and journalist dismissals in public media. On June 22, parliament created a new National Media Council with authority to hire and fire public media managers. The council consists of five members appointed to six-year terms; three appointed by parliament, and two nominated by the opposition and appointed by the president.

Since the beginning of public media reforms in January, approximately 100 journalists have left or been dismissed from their jobs.

Libel/Slander Laws: Defamation is a criminal offense and includes publicly insulting or slandering members of parliament, government ministers, or other public officials, as well as private entities and persons. Defamation outside the media is punishable by a fine and community service. The courts rarely applied maximum penalties, and persons convicted of defamation generally faced only fines or imprisonment for up to one year. The maximum sentence for insulting the president or the nation is three years' imprisonment. While journalists have never received the maximum penalty in defamation cases, according to the Helsinki Human Rights Foundation, the risk of facing criminal charges might discourage them from addressing sensitive subjects. Moreover, media owners, particularly of small local independent newspapers, were aware that potentially large fines could threaten the financial survival of their publications. According to Ministry of Justice statistics for 2015, the latest data available, courts convicted one individual of insulting the constitutional organs of the government. In 2015 the courts fined one person for public defamation.

In August the government submitted to parliament draft legislation stating, "Whoever publicly and contrary to the facts assigns the Republic of Poland or the Polish nation the liability or responsibility for the Nazi crimes committed by the Third Reich will face a fine or imprisonment of up to three years." Government officials stated the legislation was designed to deter public use of phrases like "Polish death or concentration camps," instead of "concentration camps in occupied Poland during World War II," because such terms contradict historical truth and harm the country's good name. At year's end, the draft legislation was pending in parliament.

On April 12, the Katowice regional prosecutor questioned Polish-American Princeton University professor Jan Gross for five hours about reported complaints filed by Polish citizens regarding a September 2015 article in the German newspaper *Die Welt*, in which Gross stated that Poles had killed more Jews than Poles killed Nazis during the World War II German occupation. Gross told media the prosecutors asked if he had intended to insult Poles. In October the Katowice prosecutor assigned to the case decided to discontinue the investigation, but a supervisory prosecutor overturned the decision and instructed the line prosecutor to seek expert opinions on whether Gross's statement was offensive in nature. The prosecutorial investigation continued at year's end.

Internet Freedom

The government did not restrict or disrupt access to the internet or censor online content, and there were no credible reports that the government monitored private online communications or e-mail without appropriate legal authority. The June 10 anti-terrorism law authorizes the ABW to block websites without a prior court order in cases relating to combating, preventing, and prosecuting terrorist crimes. The process by which the law was adopted, as well as its substance, provoked controversy and criticism from NGOs, as well as from the Council of Europe. The law against defamation, which restricts freedom of speech, applies to the internet as well. In 2015, the latest year for which statistics were available, prosecutors investigated 793 hate speech cases involving the internet, compared with 624 cases in 2014. In 2015, according to data from the International Telecommunication Union, 20 percent of the population had a fixed broadband subscription, and 68 percent of the population used the internet.

Academic Freedom and Cultural Events

There were no government restrictions on academic freedom or cultural events.

b. Freedom of Peaceful Assembly and Association

Freedom of Assembly

The constitution provides for the freedoms of assembly and association, and the government generally respected these rights. The antiterrorism law of 2015 permits restrictions on public assemblies in situations of elevated terrorist threats.

On December 2, the Sejm passed amendments to the public assembly law establishing a new category of "cyclical" or recurring assemblies and introducing a 328-foot distance requirement between demonstrations and counterdemonstrations. Opposition politicians and human rights advocates immediately condemned the legislation and called on the senate to reject the amendments. The Council of Europe's human rights commissioner and the director of the Office for Democratic Institutions and Human Rights of the Organization for Security and Cooperation in Europe jointly expressed concerns the amendments could undermine freedom of assembly. On December 13, the senate passed the legislation and sent the bill to the president to sign into law. On December 29, the president referred the legislation to the Constitutional Court for review without signing it.

Freedom of Association

The constitution provides for freedom of association, and the government generally respected this right.

c. Freedom of Religion

See the Department of State's *International Religious Freedom Report* at www.state.gov/religiousfreedomreport/.

d. Freedom of Movement, Internally Displaced Persons, Protection of Refugees, and Stateless Persons

The constitution and the law provide for freedom of internal movement, foreign travel, emigration, and repatriation, and the government generally respected these rights.

Abuse of Migrants, Refugees and Stateless Persons: In addition to the guarded centers for foreigners (see section 1.d.), the government operated 11 open centers for asylum seekers with an aggregate capacity of approximately 2,000 persons in the Warsaw, Bialystok, and Lublin areas. Some incidents of gender-based violence occurred, but the Office of the UN High Commissioner for Refugees (UNHCR) reported that local response teams involving doctors, psychologists, police, and social workers addressed these cases. UNHCR and the Helsinki Human Rights Foundation reported no major or persistent problems with abuse in the centers.

The government cooperated with UNHCR and other humanitarian organizations in providing protection and assistance to internally displaced persons, refugees, returning refugees, asylum seekers, stateless persons, and other persons of concern.

Protection of Refugees

Access to Asylum: The law provides for the granting of asylum or refugee status, and the government has established a system for providing protection to refugees. Each person who arrives receives consideration for asylum if requested. According to authorities, Ukrainians were rarely granted refugee status due to recognized options for internal flight within their country. Alternatively, authorities liberally used temporary residence and visa mechanisms to allow an almost 300 percent increase in Ukrainian authorized temporary residence since 2013, from an average 9,500 to an estimated 40,000 in 2016. During the year NGOs and media reported on the large number of entry refusals to Russian citizens from Chechnya who allegedly requested international protection but were denied entry at the border. Border guards stated those refused entry were economic migrants without a visa who wished to transit the country to Western Europe.

In 2015 the previous government agreed to relocate to the country 6,182 migrants from Africa and Middle East who were residing in Italy and Greece and to resettle 900 refugees from Lebanon and Jordan. At the end of September, no migrants or refugees were relocated or resettled under these commitments. The new government did follow through with financial commitments to the EU migrant crisis response and deployed asylum and border experts to Greece and Italy during the year. The government spoke out against the mandatory EU relocation quotas and advocated assisting refugees in countries of first asylum and strengthening EU external border security.

Safe Country of Origin/Transit: The EU's Dublin III Regulation, to which the country is subject, recognizes all EU countries as safe countries of origin and transit. The regulation also authorizes the governments of EU member states to return asylum seekers to the countries where they first entered the EU. The law permits denial of refugee status based on safe country of origin or safe country of transit but includes provisions that allow authorities to consider the protection needs of individuals with exceptional cases.

Employment: Asylum seekers are not allowed to work during the first six months of the asylum procedure. If the asylum procedure lasts longer than six months, they gain the right to work until the asylum decision is final.

<u>Access to Basic Services</u>: Asylum seekers faced language and cultural barriers, and had limited access to higher education. Children in centers for asylum seekers had free access to public education, but those placed with relatives in guarded centers for foreigners did not.

<u>Temporary Protection</u>: The government also provided temporary protection to 163 individuals who may not qualify as refugees during the first 11 months of the year.

Stateless Persons

According to UNHCR, at the end of 2014, there were 10,825 stateless persons in the country.

The law affords the opportunity to gain nationality. The Halina Niec Legal Aid Center observed in its report during the year on statelessness, however, that the government did not implement a formal procedure of identifying the stateless persons, leading to protection gaps and exposing stateless persons to many negative consequences, including detention.

UNHCR occasionally received complaints from stateless persons regarding problems with employment, mainly involving the lack of identity documents, which discouraged employers from offering employment to stateless persons.

Section 3. Freedom to Participate in the Political Process

The constitution provides citizens the ability to choose their government in free and fair periodic elections held by secret ballot and based on universal and equal suffrage.

Elections and Political Participation

<u>Recent Elections</u>: The presidential elections in May 2015 and the parliamentary elections in October 2015 were both considered free and fair.

<u>Participation of Women and Minorities</u>: No laws limit the participation of women and members of minorities in the political process, and they did participate.

Section 4. Corruption and Lack of Transparency in Government

Although the law provides criminal penalties for corruption by officials, corruption was a problem. On June 1, revisions to the Human Rights Ombudsman Law gave the ombudsman and several other public figures immunity from criminal liability and arrest without the prior permission of parliament. The prosecutor general or, in private lawsuits, the plaintiff's lawyer must file the motion for lifting immunity. On October 21, parliament voted to lift the immunity of Supreme Audit Commission head Krzysztof Kwiatkowski in a long-running investigation into improper public appointments. There were some reports of government corruption during the year.

Corruption: On June 22, the CBA detained regional prosecutor and former head of the Appeals Prosecutor's Office Anna H. (name protected under privacy laws) on charges of accepting bribes and abuse of power following a disciplinary court final decision to remove her from office.

Financial Disclosure: Various laws oblige elected and appointed public officials to submit financial statements about their financial assets, real property, stocks, and bonds. According to the Stefan Batory Foundation, an NGO, CBA verification was ineffective, because the agency was able to screen less than 1 percent of all financial disclosure statements filed by politicians and high-level government officials. With the exception of certain situations provided for by law, the regulations protect information included in financial statements as "restricted access" information that may be made public only with the written permission of the provider. Different laws provide for different penalties for nondisclosure.

Public Access to Information: The constitution and law provide for public access to government information, and the government generally provided such access to citizens and noncitizens, including foreign media.

Section 5. Governmental Attitude Regarding International and Nongovernmental Investigation of Alleged Violations of Human Rights

A number of domestic and international human rights groups generally operated without government restriction, investigating and publishing their findings on human rights cases.

The United Nations or Other International Bodies: After months of questioning its objectivity, on October 16, the government announced it would end its cooperation with the Venice Commission concerning the commission's critical October 14 opinion on the government's July legislative framework for the Constitutional Tribunal.

<u>Government Human Rights Bodies</u>: The law entrusts the human rights defender and the government plenipotentiary for civil society and equal treatment with the task of "implementing the principle of equal treatment."

The country's independent human rights defender processes complaints, conducts investigations, institutes and participates in court proceedings, undertakes studies, provides other public bodies with advice, proposes legislative initiatives, conducts campaigns, and cooperates with NGOs. The human rights defender has no authority to mediate disputes between private entities, even in cases of racial discrimination. The human rights defender presents an annual report to the Sejm on the state of human rights and civic freedom in the country and in 2015 reported receiving 57,627 cases.

During the annual report in September, members of the governing Law and Justice (PiS) Party strongly criticized the defender for intervening in cases related to LGBTI persons.

In his report on June 15, the Council of Europe's human rights commissioner reiterated calls made by the council's Committee on the Prevention of Torture, Committee on the Prevention of Racism and Intolerance, and the UN Committee on the Elimination of Discrimination against Women to increase the budget of the human rights defender. In 2015 the budget of the defender's office was 38.6 million zloty ($9.79 million). The defender asked for an increase of 18 percent in the 2016 budget to 35.6 million zloty ($9.03 million). In February parliament reduced the defender's general budget by 8 percent. In addition the budget for monitoring the implementation of equal treatment and for supporting victims of discrimination was cut by 30 percent.

The government plenipotentiary for civil society and equal treatment has a mandate to counter discrimination and promote equal opportunity for all. The plenipotentiary implements the government's equal treatment policy, develops and evaluates draft acts, analyzes and evaluates legal solutions, and monitors the situation within the scope of application of the principle of equal treatment. The plenipotentiary is subordinate to the prime minister's office, did not have the same institutional independence as the human rights defender, and did not have a separate budget. According to many NGOs, the government plenipotentiary was ineffective in promoting equal treatment.

Both chambers of parliament have committees on human rights and the rule of law. The committees serve a primarily legislative function and are composed of representatives from multiple political parties.

Section 6. Discrimination, Societal Abuses, and Trafficking in Persons

Women

<u>Rape and Domestic Violence</u>: Rape, including spousal rape, is illegal and punishable by up to 12 years in prison. Stalking is punishable by up to 10 years in prison. According to national police statistics, through June, there were 741 reported cases of rape. NGOs estimated that the actual number of rapes was much higher because women often were unwilling to report incidents due to social stigma. During the same period, police concluded 278 possible rape cases and forwarded them to prosecutors for indictment, and they forwarded another 36 to family courts (for underage offenders) for indictment.

While courts may sentence a person convicted of domestic violence to a maximum of five years in prison, most of those found guilty received suspended sentences. The law permits authorities to place restraining orders without prior approval from a court on spouses to protect against abuse, but police do not have the authority to issue immediate restraining orders at the scene of an incident.

During the first half of the year, police identified 7,178 cases of domestic violence. During the same period, police concluded 4,767 investigations and forwarded them to prosecutors for indictment. Through June police registered 36,855 "blue card procedures," meaning either a police officer intervened in a domestic violence situation or a police officer on duty interviewed a potential victim of domestic violence.

According to some women's organizations, the statistics understated the number of women affected by domestic violence, particularly in small towns and villages. The Women's Rights Center reported that police were occasionally reluctant to intervene in domestic violence incidents if the perpetrator was a police officer or if victims were unwilling to cooperate. In his report the human rights commissioner of the Council of Europe stated, "Women victims of domestic violence and gender-based violence are still confronted with gender bias on the part of medical staff, police, prosecutors, and judges."

The law requires every municipality in the country to set up an interagency team of experts to deal with domestic violence. According to some NGOs, this requirement might actually worsen the situation because the interagency teams focused on resolving the "family problem" rather than initially treating claims of domestic violence as criminal matters. The NGOs also believed the additional work required by the procedures discouraged police from classifying cases as domestic violence and might have contributed to a possible reduction in reported cases during the year.

Centers for victims of domestic violence operated throughout the country. In 2015, the most recent year for which statistics were available, local governments provided victims and their families with legal and psychological assistance and operated 220 crisis intervention centers and 13 shelters for pregnant women and mothers with small children. In addition local governments operated 35 specialized centers funded by the government's National Program for Combating Domestic Violence. The centers provided social, medical, psychological, and legal assistance to victims; training for personnel who worked with victims; and "corrective education" programs for abusers.

The government supports 35 specialized centers for victims of domestic abuse and corrective education programs for abusers and training for social workers, police officers, and specialists who were the first responders for victims of domestic violence.

Sexual Harassment: The law prohibits sexual harassment, and violations carry penalties of up to three years in prison. The law defines sexual harassment as discriminatory behavior in the workplace, including physical, verbal, and nonverbal acts violating an employee's dignity.

According to the Women's Rights Center, sexual harassment continued to be a serious and underreported problem. Many victims did not report abuse or withdrew harassment claims in the course of police investigations due to shame or fear of losing their job. Through June police reported 47 cases of sexual harassment, compared with 29 cases during the first six months of 2015.

Reproductive Rights: The government generally recognized the basic rights of couples and individuals to decide freely and responsibly the number, spacing, and timing of their children; manage their reproductive health; and have access to the information and means to do so, free from discrimination, coercion, or violence. While there were no restrictions on the right to obtain contraceptives, some NGOs believed their use was limited because the government excluded prescription contraceptives from its list of subsidized medicines, which made them less affordable. Some NGOs also believed that religious factors, such as the strong influence of the Roman Catholic Church, affected the use of contraceptives. The Council of Europe's human rights commissioner stated that, in addition, the law's clause of conscientious objection, invoked by some doctors who refused to prescribe and some pharmacists who refused to deliver contraceptive devices, hindered women's access to contraception. NGOs reported that refusals of reproductive health-care services continued to be very frequent and that women were often unable to find a health-care provider willing to deliver these services. The law does not permit voluntary sterilization. According to the Center for Reproductive Rights, sexuality-related counseling services for young persons were not available.

Discrimination: The constitution provides for the same legal status and rights for men and women and prohibits discrimination against women, although few laws exist to implement the provision. The constitution requires equal pay for equal work, but discrimination against women in employment existed (see section 7.d.).

The plenipotentiary for civil society and equal treatment has a mandate to counter discrimination and promote equal opportunity for all.

Children

Birth Registration: A child acquires citizenship at birth if at least one parent is a citizen, regardless of where the birth took place. Children born or found in the country whose parents were unknown or stateless are also citizens. The government has a system of universal birth registration immediately after birth.

Child Abuse: There were reports of child abuse, but convictions were rare. A government ombudsman for children's rights issued periodic reports on problems affecting children, such as the need for improved medical care for children with chronic diseases. The ombudsman's office also operated a 24-hour free hotline for abused children. In 2015 the ombudsman received 49,674 complaints of infringements of children's rights. Of those complaints, approximately 50 percent concerned the right to be brought up in a family (citing factors such as limitation of parental rights through divorce and the need for better material support for foster families), 17 percent concerned the right to education, 12 percent concerned the right to life and protection of health, 10 percent concerned the right to protection against abuse, 7 percent concerned the right to adequate social conditions, and 4 percent concerned other problems. The government operated several huge advertising campaigns, including the "You can help--React! Report!" campaign aimed at preventing sexual abuse of children and "Beating. Time to stop it" campaign aimed at preventing physical violence against children.

Early and Forced Marriage: The country's legal minimum age of marriage is 18, although the guardianship court may grant permission for girls as young as age 16 to marry under certain circumstances.

Sexual Exploitation of Children: The law prohibits sexual intercourse with children younger than 15. The penalty for statutory rape ranges from two to 12 years' imprisonment. According to the Ministry of Justice, in 2014, the most recent year for which statistics were available, courts convicted 610 persons of sexual intercourse with persons under age 15 and 12 persons of pimping minors.

Child pornography is also illegal. The production, possession, storage, or importation of child pornography involving children younger than 15 is punishable by imprisonment for a period of three months to 10 years. During the year police conducted several nationwide operations against child pornography and pedophiles. Information from authorities in other countries was usually the basis for nationwide operations. Successful prosecution of child pornography remained a challenge due to both the international nature of computer-based crimes and the difficulty of identifying perpetrators.

According to the government and the Children Empowerment Foundation, a leading NGO dealing with trafficking in children, trafficking in children for sexual exploitation remained a problem.

International Child Abductions: The country is a party to the 1980 Hague Convention on the Civil Aspects of International Child Abduction. See the Department of State's *Annual Report on International Parental Child Abduction* at travel.state.gov/content/childabduction/en/legal/compliance.html.

Anti-Semitism

The Union of Jewish Communities estimated the Jewish population at approximately 20,000. Anti-Semitic incidents continued to occur, often involving desecration of significant property, including synagogues and Jewish cemeteries. Hate speech remained a problem, as in July when Ryszard Petru, the non-Jewish leader of the Nowoczesna (Modern) political party received an anti-Semitic death threat.

In July comments by Minister of Education Anna Zalewska appeared to deny Polish responsibility for the 1942 Jedwabne and 1946 Kielce pogroms. Government officials described her remarks as unfortunate and misunderstood, stating Minister Zalewska in a subsequent print media interview acknowledged Poles had committed both atrocities. Nevertheless, critics argued the minister's comments reflected government actions that politicized a period of Polish history that demands an accurate and objective reckoning.

On February 17, a Radio Maryja commentator made anti-Semitic comments during a broadcast. On July 7, the National Radio and Television Broadcasting Council sent a letter to the head of the Redemptorist Order in Warsaw criticizing Radio Maryja for broadcasting anti-Semitic remarks and requesting the radio station not promote anti-Semitic and discriminatory content.

Xenophobic behavior and demonstrations sometimes occurred during sporting events. On August 19, 50 Lodz Widzew sports club soccer fans held a banner over a bridge that read, "19.08., today the Jews got a name. Let them burn," followed by an obscenity. The fans then burned three effigies representing Jews. By the end of September, authorities were investigating but had taken no action against any of the fans involved.

On September 28, the Wroclaw local court began a trial of a man who burned an effigy of an Orthodox Jew during a November 2015 anti-immigrant march in Wroclaw. On November 21, the court sentenced the man to 10-months' imprisonment for public incitement to hatred on religious grounds, despite the prosecutor's request for 10-months' community service. At year's end, the sentence was under appeal.

In April, two individuals who destroyed 24 tombstones at a Jewish cemetery in the town of Bielsko-Biala in November 2015 pleaded guilty.

In January, Holocaust survivors, politicians, and religious leaders gathered to mark International Holocaust Remembrance Day and commemorate the 71st anniversary of the liberation of Auschwitz-Birkenau. In July, President Andrzej Duda spoke at the 70th anniversary commemoration of a massacre of Jews in Kielce.

Trafficking in Persons

See the Department of State's *Trafficking in Persons Report* at
www.state.gov/j/tip/rls/tiprpt/.

Persons with Disabilities

The law prohibits discrimination against persons with physical, sensory,
intellectual, or mental disabilities in employment, education, air travel and other
transportation, access to health care, the judicial system, and the provision of other
government services. While the government effectively enforced these provisions,
there were reports of some societal discrimination against persons with disabilities.
The government restricted the right of persons with certain mental disabilities to
vote or participate in civic affairs.

The law states that buildings should be accessible for persons with disabilities, and
at least three laws require retrofitting of existing buildings to provide accessibility.
Many buildings remained inaccessible to persons with disabilities, because
regulations do not specify what constitutes an accessible building. Public
buildings and transportation generally were accessible, although older trains and
vehicles were often less accessible to persons with disabilities, and many train
stations were not fully accessible.

National/Racial/Ethnic Minorities

A number of xenophobic and racist incidents occurred during the year. The NGOs
Never Again and Open Republic reported a noticeable increase in the total number
of hate crimes, pointing out that, although perpetrators mainly used hate speech in
the past, during 2015 there were also violent attacks. On November 7, the National
Prosecutor's Office reported hate crimes investigated by the National Prosecutor's
office had risen 13 percent in the first six months of the year.

Prosecutors investigated 1,548 cases of hate crimes, including hate speech, in
2015, compared with 1,365 in 2014. Of these, 793 cases involved the internet, 160
cases were racist graffiti on walls or buildings, monuments and graves, 118
referred to making verbal threats to other persons, 86 cases were related to the use
of violence against other persons, 44 involved bodily injury, 39 occurred at
demonstrations or assemblies, 31 involved beating by more than one person, 29
involved sports fans or athletes, 25 involved offensive, harmful or embarrassing
physical contact, 15 involved press and book publications, eight concerned

television and radio programs, and two involved arson. Information on the remaining 198 hate crimes was unavailable.

On February 29, a Poznan local court sentenced two men to prison terms of three months and two years for beating a Syrian national in November 2015. On July 26, the court sentenced a third man to two years of community work for inciting the other two men to beat the Syrian. The court declared that the beating was a purely racist attack.

On June 23, Lodz prosecutors charged a 37-year-old man with racism, discrimination, and causing bodily harm to a 25-year old Algerian female student whom he verbally and physically attacked in the city of Lodz.

On September 8, a man physically attacked a university professor because he was speaking German while riding on a Warsaw tram. The attacker demanded the professor stop speaking German in his presence. When the professor refused, the man hit him in the face and fled the scene. On October 10, police arrested the suspected attacker and placed him in pretrial detention for three months.

Societal discrimination against Roma continued to be a problem. The 2011 national census recorded 16,723 Roma, although an official government report on the Romani community estimated that 20,000-25,000 Roma resided in the country. Romani community representatives estimated that 30,000-35,000 Roma resided in the country.

On April 21, unknown perpetrators destroyed a monument in memory of Roma shot by Nazis during World War II in Borzecin. The perpetrators split the wooden monument into pieces with an axe. By the end of September, no police investigation details were available.

In February, Czchow municipal authorities protested the resettlement of Romani community members after municipal authorities from neighboring Limanowa purchased and renovated property in Czchow to resettle three Romani families living in a dilapidated building in Limanowa. Czchow municipal authorities argued they had no experience or resources for integrating Roma, and the families remained in their Limanowa residence.

Romani leaders complained of widespread discrimination in employment, housing, banking, the justice system, the media, and education.

On January 25, a Romanian Romani group sued Poland in the European Court of Human Rights, arguing that the government violated the European Convention on Human Rights by dismantling their illegal settlement in Wroclaw in July 2015. Wroclaw city authorities destroyed the illegal settlement present in the city since 2009 without advance notification to the inhabitants who lost personal belongings when the buildings were destroyed. At year's end, the case was pending before the court.

According to the Ministry of Internal Affairs and Administration, 2,360 Romani children between ages six and 16 attended school. During the year the government allocated 10 million zloty ($2.5 million) for programs to support Roma, including for educational programs. In addition the Ministry of Education allocated 700,000 zloty ($178,000) for school equipment for Romani children. The Ministry of Internal Affairs and Administration provided 540,000 zloty ($140,000) in school grants for Romani high school and university students, postgraduate studies on Romani culture and history in Krakow, and Romani-related cultural and religious events.

While at the national level approximately 80 percent of Roma were unemployed, levels of unemployment in some regions reached nearly 100 percent.

There were isolated incidents of racially motivated violence, including verbal and physical abuse, directed at persons of African, Asian, or Arab descent. On September 10, a man verbally attacked two Asian women on a metro train in Warsaw shouting, "Poland is only for Poles" and telling them to leave the country. Police detained the perpetrator.

The Ukrainian and Belarusian minorities continued to experience petty harassment and discrimination. On June 26, approximately 20 individuals tried to disrupt the religious procession of Greek Catholic and Orthodox Church members who were marching from the local cathedral to the military cemetery to commemorate the Ukrainian soldiers who fought for Poland in 1918-1920. On June 27, police charged nine persons with violating the right to public religious practices, which carries a punishment of up to two years' imprisonment. On December 19, the Przemysl prosecutor's office indicted 19 individuals for malicious disruption of a religious procession, which carries a possible penalty of up to three years' imprisonment.

Extremist groups, while small in number, maintained a public presence in high-profile marches and on the internet, and disrupted lectures or debates on issues

they opposed. Red Watch, a webpage run by the neo-Nazi group Blood and
Honor, listed by name "traitors of the race," politicians, activists, and
representatives of left-wing organizations. The entries often included the home
addresses and telephone numbers of the persons listed. Authorities stated they
could not do anything, since the site's servers were located outside the country.

**Acts of Violence, Discrimination, and Other Abuses Based on Sexual
Orientation and Gender Identity**

While the constitution does not prohibit discrimination on the specific grounds of
sexual orientation, it prohibits discrimination "for any reason whatsoever." The
laws on discrimination in employment cover sexual orientation and gender
identity, but hate crime and incitement laws do not. Persons who want to change
their gender must sue their parents. The prime minister's plenipotentiary for civil
society and equal treatment monitors LGBTI problems.

NGOs and politicians reported increasing acceptance of LGBTI persons by society
but also stated that discrimination was still common in schools, workplaces,
hospitals, and clinics. There were some reports of skinhead violence and societal
discrimination against LGBTI persons, but NGOs maintained that most cases went
unreported.

Unknown perpetrators vandalized the offices of two LGBTI organizations. In
February perpetrators attempted to break into Lambda's Warsaw office and painted
offensive words on the office door. In April unknown perpetrators smashed office
windows of Campaign against Homophobia after unsuccessfully trying to force
entry into the building. The government's plenipotentiary for civil society and
equal treatment condemned the attacks. Police investigated but could not identify
the perpetrators.

In July the Lodz local court imposed a 200-zloty ($51) fine on an employee of a
printing house who refused services to the LGBT Business Forum foundation,
arguing he would not contribute to the promotion of LGBTI movements. The
court administratively ruled the refusal of services a misdemeanor. On July 27, the
justice minister/prosecutor general declared the court's conviction a violation of
the freedom of conscience, economic freedom, and common sense. The printer
appealed the court decision, and the case remained pending at year's end.

According to a survey by the Campaign against Homophobia in August, almost 30
percent of LGBTI persons reported having been the victims of physical or

psychological violence during the last five years. The report stated LGBTI individuals were two times more likely than the rest of society to be victims of crimes, and transgender persons were at the greatest risk with as many as half of transgender persons reporting they were victims of crime.

The police advisor for equal treatment and the human rights defender cooperated to publish a special handbook for police that promoted officers' tolerance and understanding of diversity and counseled police officers on how to work with victims of various minorities, including LGBTI individuals.

On February 25, the Supreme Court ruled that same-sex couples could be classified as cohabitants. Under the criminal law, a person closest to the accused may refuse to testify and is entitled to other legal protection. The Supreme Court ruled that legal protection could not differentiate with respect to gender.

HIV and AIDS Social Stigma

The government's AIDS center received no complaints of discrimination from HIV-positive persons during the first six months of the year.

Other Societal Violence or Discrimination

During the first months of the year, various groups organized anti-immigrant marches in several towns and cities including Bialystok, Gora Kalwaria, Biala Podlaska, Warsaw, and Lodz.

On February 18, the Lublin local court sentenced a 30-year-old woman to two months' imprisonment (suspended for two years) and 800-zloty ($203) fine for posting hateful comments regarding Syrian refugees on her Facebook page. The court ruled that she was guilty of inciting hatred on racial and national grounds and public offense of persons of Syrian origin.

On June 28, a Poznan local court sentenced a soccer fan to seven months' community work and a 3,000-zloty ($760) fine for inciting fans to shout anti-Islamic slogans during a September 2015 soccer match in the city of Poznan.

Section 7. Worker Rights

a. Freedom of Association and the Right to Collective Bargaining

The law provides for the rights of workers to form and join independent trade unions, bargain collectively, and conduct legal strikes. The law prohibits antiunion discrimination, and provides legal measures under which workers fired for union activity may demand reinstatement. There are several legal restrictions to these rights. The law does not provide for the right to form a union to persons who entered into an employment relationship based on a civil law contract, or to persons who were self-employed. In June 2015 the Constitutional Court ruled that any limitation to the freedom of association violates the constitution and required the government and parliament to amend the law on trade unions, but as of September 30, the government had not revised the law. Members in senior-level positions in the civil service cannot hold office in worker organizations.

Government workers, including police officers, border guards, prison guards, and employees of the supreme audit office, are limited to a single union. Workers in services deemed essential, such as security forces, the Supreme Chamber of Audit, police, border guards, and fire brigades, do not have the right to strike. These workers have the rights to protest and to seek resolution of their grievances through mediation and the court system.

Trade unions are registered when at least 10 eligible persons adopt a resolution to form a trade union. Newly established trade unions must appoint a founding committee consisting of three to seven persons. A new trade union must register with the National Court Registry within 30 days of the resolution. The court may remove a trade union from the registry only if a trade union adopts resolution to dissolve, is no longer able to operate due to the bankruptcy, liquidation, or reorganization of the company in which the trade union operated, or if a trade union has fewer than 10 members for more than three months.

Legal strikes require the support of at least 50 percent of all employees in a company or industry-level vote. To allow for required mediation, a strike may not be called fewer than 14 days after workers present their demands to an employer. The law obligates employers to notify the district inspection office in their region about a group dispute in the workplace. Cumbersome procedures made it difficult for workers to meet all of the technical requirements for a legal strike. What constitutes a strike under the labor law is limited to strikes regarding wages and working conditions. The law prohibits collective bargaining for key civil servants, appointed or elected employees of state and municipal bodies, court judges, and prosecutors.

The penalties for obstructing trade union activity range from fines to community service. The government did not effectively enforce applicable laws. Resources, inspections, and remediation efforts were not adequate, and the small fines imposed as punishment were an ineffective deterrent to employers. Administrative and judicial procedures were subject to lengthy delays and appeals. Unions alleged that the government did not consistently enforce laws prohibiting retribution against strikers. In 2015 the National Labor Inspectorate (NLI) registered 1,202 disputes regarding working conditions, social benefits, and the right to freedom of trade union activity, filed under collective bargaining rules as a prerequisite for striking.

Violations of freedom of association and the right to collective bargaining occurred. While many workers exercised the right to organize and join unions, many small- and medium-sized firms, which employed a majority of the workforce, discriminated against those who attempted to organize.

Labor leaders continued to report that employers regularly discriminated against workers who attempted to organize or join unions, particularly in the private sector. Discrimination typically took the forms of intimidation, termination of work contracts without notice, and closing of the workplace. Some employers sanctioned employees who tried to organize unions. The International Trade Union Confederation reported allegations of discrimination against members of the Independent Self-Governing Trade Union Solidarity "Solidarnosc" in Pyrzyce. These allegations included dismissals of six union members due to their affiliation with this union.

b. Prohibition of Forced or Compulsory Labor

The law prohibits all forms of forced or compulsory labor. Nevertheless, forced labor occurred.

While the government effectively enforced the law, there were some limitations with respect to identification of victims of forced labor and distinguishing between forced labor and working conditions violations. Penalties for forced labor violations ranged from three to 15 years' imprisonment and sufficiently stringent to deter violations compared to other serious crimes. In 2015, the last year for which statistics were available, the government assisted in removing 114 victims from forced labor.

There were reports that foreign and domestic men were subjected to forced labor in the agricultural, manufacturing, and food processing sectors and that men, women, and children were subjected to forced begging.

Also see the Department of State's *Trafficking in Persons Report* at www.state.gov/j/tip/rls/tiprpt/.

c. Prohibition of Child Labor and Minimum Age for Employment

The law prohibits the employment of children under age 16, with exceptions in the cultural, artistic, sporting, and advertising fields when parents or guardians and the local labor inspector give their permission. Persons between ages 16 and 18 may work only if they have completed middle school, if the proposed employment constitutes vocational training, and if the work is not harmful to their health.

The government effectively enforced these laws in the formal sector, but the NLI was not empowered to inspect private farms or homes. During the first half of the year, the inspectorate conducted 710 inspections involving underage employees (ages 16 to 18). Authorities levied fines totaling 91,350 zloty ($23,179) in 270 cases. Trade unions generally argue that fines imposed on employers for workers' rights violations were too small and ineffective.

The NLI reported that many employers underpaid minors or delayed their pay. The majority of employees ages 16 and 17 worked in commercial enterprises and repairs shops, processing industries, restaurants, and construction. Some children under age 18 also engaged in hazardous work in agriculture, primarily on family farms. Migrant Romani children from Romania were subjected to forced begging. Commercial sexual exploitation of children also occurred (see section 6).

d. Discrimination with Respect to Employment and Occupation

The law prohibits discrimination with respect to employment or occupation in any way, directly or indirectly, on the grounds of race, sex, color, religion, political opinion, national origin, ethnic origin, disability, sexual orientation, age, trade union membership, and regardless of whether the person is hired for definite or indefinite contracts, or for full- or half-time work. The law does not specifically prohibit such discrimination based on language, HIV-positive status, gender identity, or social status. The government did not effectively enforce these laws and regulations. According to the Polish Society for Antidiscrimination Law, by law the accused must prove that discrimination did not take place, but judges often placed the burden on the victim to prove that discrimination occurred.

Discrimination in employment and occupation occurred with respect to gender, age, minority status, disability, political opinion, sexual orientation and gender identity, and HIV-positive status. According to a European Commission report, the gender wage gap in 2013, the latest year for which data were available, was 6.4 percent. The Main Statistical Office's 2016 gender pay gap report stated women earned 7.7 percent less than men earned in 2014. The report attributed the remuneration gap primarily to differing job qualifications. Discrimination against Romani workers also occurred (see section 6).

e. Acceptable Conditions of Work

The national monthly minimum wage, which took effect in January, was 1,850 zloty ($469). On August 8, the president signed a law establishing 12 zloty ($3) as the minimum hourly wage to cover formal and informal work agreements. The law is to take effect January 2017. According to the Institute of Labor and Social Studies, in 2015 the social minimum monthly income level was 1,079 zloty ($274) for one person and 3,421 zloty ($868) for a family of four. In 2015 the subsistence level, which is the bare amount needed to cover the costs of housing and food, was 546 zloty ($139) for one person and 1,856 zloty ($471) for a family of four.

The law provides for a standard workweek of 40 hours, with an upper limit of 48 hours including overtime. It requires premium pay for overtime. It prohibits excessive or compulsory overtime and sets a maximum of 150 hours of overtime per year. The law provides for workers to receive at least 11 hours of uninterrupted rest per day and 35 hours of uninterrupted rest per week. The constitution provides every employee the right to statutorily specified days free from work as well as annual paid holidays. The law also provides for 20 days of paid annual leave for employees with fewer than 10 years of employment and 26 days for those employed at least 10 years.

The law defines strict and extensive minimum conditions to protect worker health and safety, and empowers the NLI to supervise and monitor implementation of worker health and safety laws and to close workplaces with unsafe conditions. Workers could remove themselves from situations that endangered health or safety without jeopardy to their employment, and authorities effectively protected employees in this situation. The NLI's powers are limited to the formal economy;

it does not have authority to monitor implementation of worker health and safety laws in the informal economy, private farms, and households.

Authorities did not effectively enforce minimum wage, hours of work, and occupational health and safety in the formal or informal sectors. Resources, inspections, and remediation efforts were inadequate. In 2015 there were approximately 1,700 labor inspectors, the same number as in 2014.

According to the inspectorate's 2015 report, the most frequent labor rights violations concerned failure to pay or delayed payment of wages. Most wage payment violations occurred in the services, construction, and processing industries. Seasonal workers were particularly vulnerable to such violations. The national inspectorate's report did not cover domestic workers because inspectors could only conduct inspections in businesses, not private homes. The second-most common problem was inaccurate timekeeping records for hours worked.

Employers often ignored requirements regarding overtime pay. A large percentage of construction workers and seasonal agricultural laborers from Ukraine and Belarus earned less than the minimum wage. The large size of the informal economy--particularly in the construction and transportation industries--and the low number of government labor inspectors made enforcement of the minimum wage difficult. The Main Statistical Office definition of informal economy includes unregistered employment performed without a formal contract or agreement, and is not counted as a contribution to social security and from which income taxes are not deducted. According to Main Statistical Office, in 2014 (the latest year for which data were available), approximately 4.5 percent of workforce (711,000 persons) worked in the informal economy.

Trade union leaders stated penalties for employers were not sufficient to deter violations. In the case of serious violations, labor inspectors may submit the case to a court, which may impose a fine of up to 30,000 zloty ($7,600). According to labor laws, persons who maliciously violate the labor rights of employees may face up to two years' imprisonment. According to the NLI, employers implemented 95 percent of all labor-inspection decisions, although a report by the NLI indicated that some legal restrictions, such as the requirement in some sectors that a company receive seven days' advance notification of upcoming inspections, weakened the effectiveness of labor inspections. International observers noted that the NLI's mandate to both confirm the legal status of workers and monitor working conditions creates a potential conflict of interest.

During 2015 the NLI continued a "Safety at Work Depends on You" campaign targeting employees and employers in high-risk sectors, such as industrial processing companies (mining and metalworking). The campaign took the form of training and information briefings, television and radio commercials broadcast on both private and public television and radio stations, and postings on the internet. In addition the NLI organized a prevention and information campaign targeting small construction companies, which included training on work safety standards for employees and employers. The NLI also continued a specific information and preventive program in construction, and offered training for small enterprises (those hiring up to 49 employees). The NLI also continued a television and radio campaign, "Respect Life! Safe Work on Farms," targeting individual farmers and family members. The NLI visited many private farms to assess safety conditions and organized a number of competitions for individual farmers.

In June 2015 the NLI launched a new public-awareness campaign, "Before you start," targeting mainly senior high-school and university students to inform them regarding their labor rights. In cooperation with the Central Institute of Labor Protection, senior high schools, educational authorities, universities, local governments and trade unions, the NLI continued an educational program called "Safety Culture" to instruct senior high-school and university students about workplace safety and to promote general knowledge about labor law.

In the first half of the year, the Central Statistical Office reported 39,233 victims of workplace accidents, an increase of 2,122 from the same period in 2015. The highest number of victims worked in industrial processing, the retail and wholesale trade, the health service sector, transportation, warehouse management, and construction. In 2015 the inspectorate investigated 2,024 accidents in which there were deaths or injuries, including 272 workers killed and 709 persons seriously injured. The NLI reported that, as in previous years, most of the fatal accidents occurred in the industrial-processing and construction industries. Employers routinely exceeded standards limiting exposure to chemicals, dust, and noise. According to the inspectorate's 2015 report, inadequate training of employees, the poor quality of job-related risk assessment tools, and inadequate measures by employers to prevent accidents were the leading causes of workplace accidents.